HISTORIC COMMUNITIES

Pioneer Recipes

Bobbie Kalman & Lynda Hale

Illustrations by Barbara Bedell

🌳 Crabtree Publishing Company

www.crabtreebooks.com

HISTORIC
COMMUNITIES

Created by Bobbie Kalman

Thanks to my Mom, Leila Hale
for instilling in me
the passion for food and cooking

Editor-in-Chief
Bobbie Kalman

Writing team
Bobbie Kalman
Lynda Hale
Hannelore Sotzek

Managing editor
Lynda Hale

Editors
Heather Levigne
John Crossingham

Computer design
Lynda Hale

Consultant
Ellen Brown, Founding Food Editor
of USA *Today* and author of several
best-selling cookbooks

Printer
Worzalla Publishing Company

Special thanks to
Genessee Country Museum, Colonial Williamsburg Foundation, Fort George,
Black Creek Pioneer Village/TRCA, Environment Canada, Ellen Brown,
Kevin Spicer, Leigh Adamson, Brian Adamson, Jaimie Carini, Lisa Cooper,
The Complete Farmer, The Complete Home

Photographs
Black Creek Pioneer Village/TRCA: pages 5, 11; Jim Bryant: pages 24 (top),
27 (bottom); Colonial Williamsburg Foundation: pages 10, 21; Marc Crabtree:
page 12; Marc Crabtree at Black Creek Pioneer Village: page 6; Marc Crabtree
at Fort George: pages 17, 20; Marc Crabtree at Genessee County Museum:
pages 7, 22, 24 (bottom); Digital Stock: page 27 (top); Environment Canada.
Canadian Parks Service, Ontario Region: pages 8, 26; David Schimpky at
Genessee Country Museum: page 25

Illustrations, Colorizations, and Reproductions
All illustrations by Barbara Bedell, except the following:
Antoinette "Cookie" Bortolon: pages 15 (bottom), 17; Giraudon/Art Resource,
NY: page 28 (top) (detail); John Mantha: back cover; Trevor Morgan: page 6;
Bonna Rouse: pages 4 (top), 19, 30 (bottom)

Digital Prepress
Best Graphics Int'l Co.; Embassy Graphics (cover)

Crabtree Publishing Company
www.crabtreebooks.com   1-800-387-7650

Cataloguing in Publication Data
Kalman, Bobbie
   Pioneer Recipes

p. cm. —(Historic communities series)
Includes index.
ISBN 0-86505-438-X (library bound) ISBN 0-86505-468-1 (pbk.)
This book presents information on pioneeer cookery and instructions for recipies prepared in the
spirit of the pioneers, including multicultural dishes, historical methods, and current adaptations.
1. Cookery, North America—History—19th century—Juvenile literature. 2. Frontier and pioneer
life—North America—History—19th century—Juvenile literature. 3. Food habits—North
America—History—19th century—Juvenile literature. [1. Cookery, North American—History—
19th century. 2. Frontier and pioneer life.] I. Hale, Lynda. II. Bedell, Barbara, ill. III. Title. IV. Series:
Kalman, Bobbie. Historic Communities.
TX715.K1275 2001   j641.5973'09'034—dc21   LC00-034606
                                                                                                                CIP

Contents

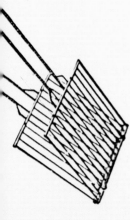
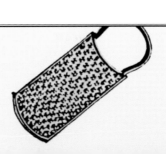

Preparing food the pioneer way

*When cooking over an open fire, pioneers hung their pots on a **lugpole**. It was made of moist, green wood so it did not burn.*

In the 1800s, thousands of people left their homes in Europe and Asia to live in North America. Many settled in wilderness areas, where their nearest neighbors were miles away.

Living off the land

There were no grocery stores for buying food. Instead, the pioneers hunted game such as bears, elk, deer, moose, beavers, rabbits, and squirrels. Turkeys, pheasant, and other wild birds also made tasty meals. Rivers, lakes, and oceans provided the settlers with fish. Pioneers discovered a great variety of fruits, berries, nuts, and other foods growing wild in the forests and fields.

Growing and preserving foods

The settlers cleared trees and rocks from areas of land in order to grow vegetables and grains such as corn, oats, and wheat. They raised chickens, sheep, pigs, and cows for eggs, wool, meat, and milk. Since the settlers could not grow or gather food during the winter, they **preserved** it. They dried, smoked, salted, and pickled their foods in the summer and autumn to make them last through the cold months.

The essential fireplace

The pioneers relied on the kitchen fireplace for cooking, heating, and as a source of light. Many fireplaces had a bread oven built into the side for baking. Some settlers used an outdoor oven in the summer so the house would not get overheated. Many people in the southern United States had a summer kitchen, which was located in a separate building. Eventually, iron stoves replaced the fireplace for preparing meals.

Herbs were picked in the summer and hung to dry. They were used later for seasoning food.

(above) Some settlers used a Dutch oven for baking bread, rolls, and biscuits. This large, covered pot was placed directly on the hot coals, and more coals were placed on top of the lid to heat the contents evenly.

(below) Most pioneers only had a few pieces of cookware including a frying pan, kettle, coffee pot, pans, mixing bowls, a sharp knife, and some wooden spoons.

Foods of yesterday prepared today

This book contains recipes of foods enjoyed by the pioneers who came to North America from Great Britain, Eastern and Western Europe, Scandinavia, Russia, and Asia. It also includes Native American, African American, and Mexican recipes. We still enjoy these foods today.

Making bread the pioneer way

To make bread, the pioneers mixed flour, milk, fat, sugar, salt, and yeast together in a bowl to form dough. The dough was **kneaded**, or punched and rolled, on a table. After the dough was kneaded, it was covered and placed in a warm area to **rise**, or puff up. It was then kneaded again and divided into loaves for baking. The bread was baked in a well-heated oven. The pioneers used a long-handled board called a **peel** to place the dough in the hot oven.

bread oven

The bread oven was usually located at one side of the fireplace. It was heated with coals from the fire, which were removed once the stone surface of the oven was hot. Many ovens had a metal door to keep the heat inside while the bread was baking.

(top) Bread was made almost every day. Many kitchens had a **dough box** *on which dough was kneaded.*

Milk from a cow

The milk used by pioneers came straight from a cow. After a cow was milked, the fresh milk was put into a stone container called a **crock**, which was stored in a cool room for a day or two. The cream in the milk rose to the top. The pioneers **skimmed**, or removed, the cream and put it into a separate jug, leaving behind the milk.

Making butter the old-fashioned way

To make butter, the pioneers poured cream into a **butter churn**. They **churned**, or mixed, the cream into butter using a **dasher**. Rolling the dasher from side to side and pumping it up and down caused small grains of butter to form. After churning for some time, larger pieces of butter floated in a liquid called **buttermilk**. The buttermilk was strained from the butter, and the butter was washed, drained, and salted. The pioneers pressed it into a butter mold to give it a decorative shape.

Settlers had to keep their butter churn, dasher, and utensils very clean so the cream would not spoil and ruin the taste of the butter.

dasher

butter churn

butter mold

Homemade Butter

You can make butter at home without a churn. Just fill a jar with some cream and shake, shake, shake!

2 cups (500 ml) whipping cream
clean jar with a fitted lid

1. Pour cream into the jar.
2. Shake the jar continuously to form butter.
3. Remove the solid lump of butter from the jar and wrap it in a tea towel.
4. Wring out the tea towel to remove the liquid from the butter.
5. Press the butter into a shape and set it in the refrigerator to chill and harden. Use the remaining buttermilk for cooking or drinking.

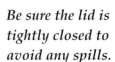

Be sure the lid is tightly closed to avoid any spills.

Use a clean, dry towel in which to wrap the butter and squeeze out the liquid.

Safety tips and cooking terms

Cookware was sturdy enough to withstand the heat of a fireplace or bread oven.

The recipes in this book come from the time of the pioneers, but we have adjusted them to use ingredients that are available today. The pioneers had to do everything from scratch, but you can use a food processor, blender, mixer, and microwave oven. In some cases, you can make the recipes even simpler by using frozen or canned foods. The dishes will still taste delicious!

Cautions:

Ask an adult for assistance when you see the following symbols alongside a recipe. Do not stand near a microwave oven when it is on!

 This recipe has ingredients that need to be chopped or shredded with a sharp knife.

 This recipe has ingredients that need to be fried in hot oil or butter on top of a stove.

 You can make this recipe more quickly if you use a food processor. Do not touch the blades!

Levels of preparation:

Each recipe is rated by the effort required to make it. The wooden spoon symbols in the information boxes will give you an idea of the work involved in preparing each recipe.

 Easy—no cooking   *Some cooking required*   *A bit more challenging*

Safety tips for the kitchen

 When working in the kitchen, make sure you have an adult with you.

 If your hair is long, tie it back so that it will not fall into the food or get in your way while cooking.

 Before handling food, wash your hands and dry them on a clean towel. Always wash your hands after handling eggs or any kind of raw meat. Make sure you rinse all fruits and vegetables thoroughly before you cook or eat them.

 To avoid spilling hot liquid on yourself or others, turn pot handles away from the edge of the stove.

 When you are finished cooking, clean the kitchen. Wash, dry, and put away any dishes, cookware, and utensils that you used. Wipe the counters clean, and sweep the floor.

Cooking terms

Cooks use a number of terms to describe how they prepare food. The terms illustrated on this page are used in the recipes throughout the book. The recipes also use short forms for measurements. For example, the letter "l" stands for liter and "ml" for milliliter. See the glossary on page 31 for more cooking terms.

slice

dice

shred

grate

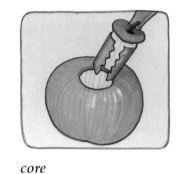

core

score

rub in

knead

pinch

strain

blend

beat

whip

purée

make drippings

simmer (cook, low heat)

toothpick test

dust

Breads and muffins

Bread was a **staple** of pioneer life. A staple is a basic food that is eaten every day. To make bread, the pioneers used flour and water or milk as well as yeast, which made the dough rise. They made flour by grinding the grains of plants such as wheat, corn, rye, or oats. Most settlers made their flour from wheat. The pioneers often traveled long distances to bring the grain they grew to a **gristmill**, where it was ground into flour. Before the gristmill was built, people had to grind their grain by hand using a **mortar** and **pestle** or a hand mill called a **quern**.

Irish Soda Bread

This bread is quick and easy to make. It will give you a taste of the kind of bread Irish settlers offered their visitors. You can replace the milk and vinegar with ½ cup (125 ml) of buttermilk.

Preparation time: 10 minutes	Servings: 4
Cooking time: 30 minutes	

½ cup (125 ml) milk
1 teaspoon (5 ml) vinegar
2 cups (500 ml) flour
1 teaspoon (5 ml) baking soda

1 teaspoon (5 ml) cream of tartar
½ teaspoon (3 ml) salt
2 tablespoons (30 ml) butter

Preheat oven to 425°F (220°C).
1. Add vinegar to milk and set aside.
2. Mix together flour, baking soda, cream of tartar, and salt.
3. Rub in butter with your fingertips.
4. Add milk mixture to flour mixture a little at a time and stir in to form the dough.
5. Shape the dough into a flat circle about 2 inches (5 cm) thick on a lightly greased cookie sheet.
6. Bake in oven for 30 minutes. Eat the bread while it is fresh and warm.

Grains were often crushed by hand. The mother and daughter above are using a mortar and pestle to grind corn to make cornmeal.

Plain Ginger Bread
"To a cup of molasses add a piece of butter the size of a large walnut, the butter being melted, put in one cup sour milk, and a teaspoonful of soda. Spice with cloves or ginger; mix in enough flour to make a thick batter, and bake slowly.
THE COMPLEAT FARMER

Frybread

Frybread is flatbread that was cooked over a fire. The Native Americans introduced it to the settlers.

Preparation time: 10 minutes	Servings: 4
Cooking time: 25 minutes	

1½ cups (375 ml) flour
1 teaspoon (5 ml) baking powder
1 tablespoon (15 ml) butter, melted
½ cup (125 ml) warm milk
pinch of salt
pinch of sugar
4 tablespoons (60 ml) vegetable oil

1. To make dough, mix all ingredients except oil in a bowl. Knead the dough until smooth and divide into four pieces. Shape each piece into a flat circle.
2. On medium heat, heat oil in a frying pan. Fry dough rounds one at a time until brown and crispy.

Basic Muffins

Use this basic recipe to make a different muffin every time! See the variations below to give you ideas.

Preparation time: 20 minutes	Servings:
Cooking time: 20 minutes	12 muffins

2 cups (500 ml) flour
½ cup (125 ml) sugar
1 tablespoon (15 ml) baking powder
½ teaspoon (3 ml) salt
¼ cup (60 ml) vegetable oil
1 cup (250 ml) milk
2 eggs

Preheat oven to 350°F (175°C). Grease muffin tins.

1. In a large bowl, combine flour, sugar, baking powder, and salt. (Add an ingredient from below.)
2. In another bowl, beat together oil, milk, and eggs.
3. Add liquid mixture to dry ingredients and blend just enough for a lumpy batter.
4. Spoon into muffin tin and fill each to ¾ full.
5. Bake for 20 minutes or until a toothpick inserted in the center of a muffin comes out clean.

Variations: To the dry ingredients, add 1 cup (250 ml) of blueberries, raspberries, peeled and finely chopped apple, chocolate chips, chopped nuts, or raisins. You can even add your choice of grated cheese!

Muffins are small, round loaves of bread. Unlike other types of bread, muffins do not require kneading or rising before baking. Many types of muffins are sweet and taste more like cake than bread.

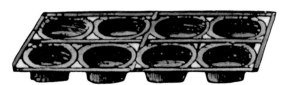

Muffin tins and other types of tinwork, such as molds, could be purchased at the general store. Peddlers also sold these useful items. They traveled from village to village selling goods from their wagon.

Topping bread

The pioneers often ate meals that consisted only of bread. To make their meal tastier and more nutritious, they topped the bread with butter or other spreads.

For breakfast, scones, muffins, and other breads were topped with **preserves** that were made when fruits were in season. Try the delights below on your favorite breakfast bread. You can substitute other berries in either of these recipes.

Apples were picked in the autumn. They were used to make jelly, apple butter, or chutney with raisins and nuts.

scone

For a quick fruit spread, blend strawberry pieces with cream cheese.

English muffin

bagel

muffin

For an easy fruit-filled muffin, use the basic recipe (page 11). Fill the cups ¹/₂ full with batter, add 1 teaspoon of this jam, and top with remaining batter.

Strawberry Butter

Preparation time: 5 minutes	Makes 1 cup
Cooking time: 5 minutes	(250 ml)

2 cups (500 ml) fresh strawberries
2 tablespoons (30 ml) water
2 tablespoons (30 ml) sugar

¹/₂ cup (125 ml) butter
2 tablespoons (30 ml) honey or maple syrup

1. Place strawberries, water, and sugar in a pot and boil for 5 minutes. Strain the mixture through a sieve into a cup. Use a spoon to press out the juices.
2. Pour strawberry liquid, butter, and honey or syrup into a food processor and purée.
3. Transfer to a small serving bowl, and refrigerate before serving.

Blueberry Jam

Preparation time: 5 minutes	Makes 2 cups
Cooking time: 15 minutes	(500 ml)

2 cups (500 ml) blueberries
¹/₄ cup (60 ml) water

2 cups (500 ml) sugar
¹/₂ teaspoon (3 ml) cinnamon

1. In a saucepan over medium heat, cook berries in water until tender (about 5 minutes).
2. Reduce heat to low, and add sugar and cinnamon. Simmer mixture. Stir continuously until jelly is thick (about 15 minutes). Cool before serving.

Lunchtime!

For lunch, bread was topped with meats, cheeses, eggs, or vegetables. Settlers used a variety of breads and toppings, depending on the country from which they came. Try some of the sandwich fillings on this page. Mix and match the toppings with different breads.

Round bread, such as pumpernickel, sourdough, and Irish soda, make great sandwiches for a group. Try a different filling on each level!

Smørrebrød

The Danish version of the sandwich was called *Smørrebrød*, which means "buttered bread." It was **open-faced**, or made with one piece of bread. Top pumpernickel bread with salmon or egg salad, cheese, and tomatoes, or your favorite topping! For a Russian-style topping, add parsley and dill to the egg salad.

When cut in half, many types of pita bread open to form a pocket. You can fill the pocket with egg, chicken, tuna, or vegetable salad. Just top the veggies with your favorite salad dressing.

Toasted Western

The Toasted Western was popular with cowboys. Whisk two eggs together and fry until cooked. Layer three pieces of toast with the egg as well as cheese, tomato, and ham or cooked bacon.

A baguette is a type of long French bread. Make one big sandwich and then slice it into many pieces.

Quesadillas

A Mexican version of a sandwich is called a *quesadilla*, which is two tortillas filled with beans, meat, cheese, and vegetables. Warm in oven and cut into fours.

Smoked Salmon Spread

Many sandwich fillings can be made quickly and easily by using a food processor or mixer. Try this Eastern European Jewish bread topper!

To make a Welsh Rarebit Fajita, place pieces of cheese and cooked ham or bacon on a tortilla. Heat in the oven until the cheese melts. Add tomato slices. Fold up the bottom of the tortilla. Then fold one side over the other.

Preparation time: 5 minutes	Makes 1 cup
Cooking time: none	(250 ml)

½ cup (125 ml) cream cheese, softened
3 slices smoked salmon

2 tablespoons (30 ml) chopped, fresh dill
juice of ½ lemon

1. Combine all ingredients in a food processor and blend until smooth.
2. Spread on your favorite bread or on a tortilla shell and roll up the shell!

Italian immigrants used bread dough to make pizza. Make your own pizza using pizza dough and your favorite ingredients, such as tomato sauce, cheese, mushrooms, onions, spinach, and bacon.

Pioneer pancakes

Pancakes were inexpensive, filling, and easy for the pioneers to make. Today we eat pancakes for breakfast, but the pioneers also ate pancakes for dinner or dessert! Settlers from different countries each had their own way of making pancakes. Flapjacks, *crêpes*, *blinis*, *blintzes*, and *palacsinta* are all pancakes! Some pancakes were made from a thick batter, and others were thin enough to be rolled with fillings inside.

Flapjacks

This is a basic recipe for thick pancakes. The word "flapjack" used to mean a pastry flap with a **jack**, or ½ cup, of fruit or berries inside. Over the years, flapjack became another name for pancake. Put the "jack" back into your flapjack and add a half cup of your favorite fruit to this recipe!

 Preparation time: 10 minutes Cooking time: 30 minutes Makes: 8 pancakes

1 cup (250 ml) flour	**1 egg, lightly beaten**
2 tablespoons (30 ml) sugar	**1 cup (250 ml) milk**
1 teaspoon (5 ml) baking powder	**3 tablespoons (45 ml) melted butter**

1. Mix together flour, sugar, and baking powder in a large bowl.
2. Beat together eggs, milk, and butter.
3. Add liquid ingredients to the dry ingredients and blend. If you are adding fruit, stir it into the batter.
4. Over medium heat, melt a little butter in a frying pan and pour enough batter to form a 5 inch (13 cm) pancake. When the pancake begins to bubble all over and the edges turn brown, flip it and cook the other side.
5. Keep the pancakes in a warm oven until you are ready to serve them.

Add the liquid a little at a time. Depending on the type of flour you use, you may not need as much liquid as called for in the recipe. If the batter is too thin, add a little bit of flour to thicken it.

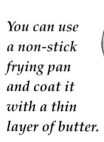

You can use a non-stick frying pan and coat it with a thin layer of butter.

Tastes galore!

Swedish pioneers served their pancakes with lingonberry jam and sprinkled them with fine sugar. British settlers squeezed lemon juice on their thin pancakes and also sprinkled sugar on top. Welsh settlers added currants to their pancakes as the pancakes were cooking. Many Eastern Europeans put fruit preserves on thin pancakes, rolled them into tubes, and sprinkled them with sugar. The French put meat and vegetables or fresh fruit and cream into thin *crêpes*. Russian *blinis* were small pancakes topped with sour cream, chopped boiled egg, and caviar or with a sweet filling.

French **crêpes** *and Hungarian* **palacsinta** *are rolled and eaten with a knife and fork.* **Crêpes** *are smaller and slightly thinner.*

Sweet Russian **blinis** *are thick pancakes. They are often filled with cottage cheese and sugar and then topped with fruit.*

Jewish **blintzes** *are filled with a cream-cheese mixture, folded, and topped with a fruit sauce.*

Sugar and other sweeteners

Sugar is made from sugar cane plants or sugar beets. It was often difficult and expensive for pioneers to purchase the type of white sugar that we use today, so other sweeteners were used instead. **Molasses** is a dark syrup that is produced when making sugar. It costs less than sugar and was often used in baking. Brown sugar was also preferred because it was less expensive than white sugar.

Dutch **waffles** *are made by heating thick pancake batter in a* **waffle iron**.

Syrups and honey

Corn syrup was another sugar substitute. It was made from **cornstarch**, which is the inner part of the kernel of corn that is ground into a fine powder. Maple syrup was made from the sap of sugar maple trees. It is a popular topping for pancakes. Many pioneers also used honey in place of sugar. It was not only spread on breads and pancakes but was often used to replace sugar in making cakes and pies.

Sugar was sold in a cone or block. The pioneers used a **sugar cutter** *to cut the cone into smaller pieces.*

A hearty bowl of porridge

A bowl of porridge was a good way to start off a day of hard work. Porridge is made by cooking grains such as oats, cornmeal, wheat, or rice in boiling milk or water. Pioneers flavored their porridge with fruit, nuts, sugar, or honey.

Irish Oatmeal

Irish settlers did not make porridge with the oat flakes that we use today. They used oat kernels. Oat kernels have a nutty taste and can be eaten hot or cold. To make Irish Oatmeal, use slow-cook oats, which are also sold as steel-cut oats.

Oats were among the crops grown by the settlers. The stalks were harvested, and the grains from the seeds were ground into oat flour or passed through rollers to make rolled oats.

Fruit and Nut Porridge

Bring 4 cups (1 l) of water to a boil and add a pinch of salt. Add 1 cup (250 ml) of oats and cook on low heat for 45 minutes, stirring often. Spoon some oatmeal into a bowl and cover with milk. Add chopped nuts, honey, maple syrup, brown sugar, cinnamon, yogurt, fresh berries, or grated apples. In fact, any kind of nut, syrup, or fresh, frozen, or dried fruit makes a delicious topping.

Overnight Oats

Another way to enjoy oats is to eat them cold. Use the same kind of oats as in the previous recipe. Before you go to bed, put ½ cup of oats in your favorite cereal bowl. Add just enough cold water to cover the oats. Place a small plate or some plastic wrap over the bowl and put it in the refrigerator. In the morning, the oats will be soft. Add milk or yogurt and any of the toppings mentioned above.

Easy Swedish Rice Cream

The Swedish settlers enjoyed a hot breakfast of rice porridge called *Skånsk gröt*. It was sweet, rich, and creamy. This is a quick version.

Preparation time: 5 minutes	Servings: 2
Cooking time: 2 minutes (optional)	

1 cup (250 ml) cooked rice
1 cup (250 ml) milk
1 apple, peeled, cored, and grated

1 teaspoon (5 ml) cinnamon
2 tablespoons (30 ml) brown sugar
¼ cup (60 ml) raisins

Combine all ingredients in a bowl. Either heat the mixture in the microwave for a minute or eat it cold.

Enjoy it again and again!

You can store leftover oatmeal in your refrigerator and use it later. Just spoon out the amount you need and cover with milk. Heat in the microwave on high for one minute. If you do not have a microwave, heat some milk in a pan and then add the oatmeal until it warms. Add your favorite toppings to your bowl.

Iron pots were hung over the fire using a series of hooks called a **trammel,** *which rested on an iron* **crane.** *The cook could swing out the crane to check the meal without having to bend over the flames.*

The **spider** *had feet that kept the pan above the coals. It also had a long handle, which made it easy to remove the pan from a fire.*

Foods from the fields and garden

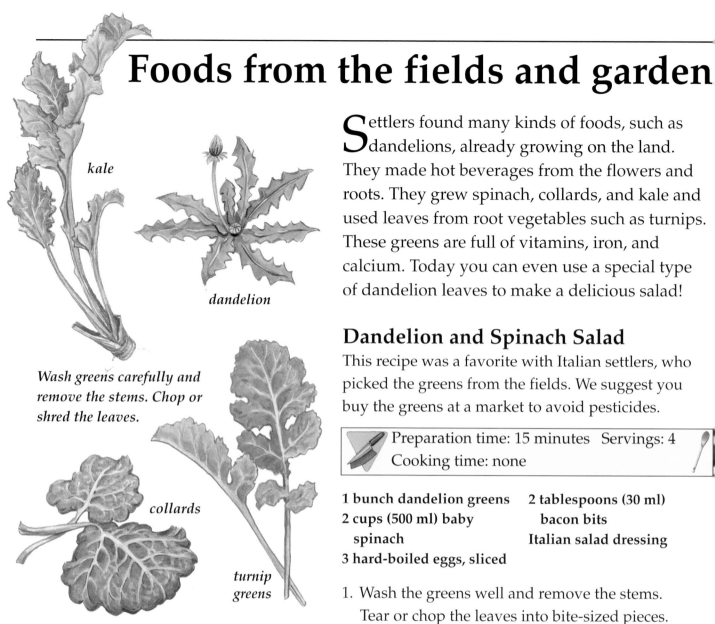

kale

dandelion

Wash greens carefully and remove the stems. Chop or shred the leaves.

collards

turnip greens

spinach

Mr. Gomez's Pea Soup
"Put the peas into water and boil about two hours, strain and put on fire; add vegetables (not cabbage) and fry half an onion to a crisp brown; small piece of ham; fry toasted bread and add in small bits." THE COMPLETE HOME

Settlers found many kinds of foods, such as dandelions, already growing on the land. They made hot beverages from the flowers and roots. They grew spinach, collards, and kale and used leaves from root vegetables such as turnips. These greens are full of vitamins, iron, and calcium. Today you can even use a special type of dandelion leaves to make a delicious salad!

Dandelion and Spinach Salad

This recipe was a favorite with Italian settlers, who picked the greens from the fields. We suggest you buy the greens at a market to avoid pesticides.

Preparation time: 15 minutes   Servings: 4
Cooking time: none

1 bunch dandelion greens	**2 tablespoons (30 ml)**
2 cups (500 ml) baby	**bacon bits**
spinach	**Italian salad dressing**
3 hard-boiled eggs, sliced	

1. Wash the greens well and remove the stems. Tear or chop the leaves into bite-sized pieces.
2. In a bowl, toss the greens with the dressing.
3. Garnish with egg slices and bacon bits.

Cooked Greens

Cooked greens were enjoyed by African American settlers. They are nutritious and very tasty!

Preparation: 10 minutes
Cooking: 2 - 20 minutes

1. Cut two strips of bacon into pieces and fry them in a large pan. Add shredded collards, spinach, kale, or turnip greens and a little water, as needed. Sprinkle with sugar to remove any bitterness.
2. Simmer on low heat until tender. Collards, kale, and turnip greens take about 20 minutes, dandelion and spinach take only 2 or 3 minutes.

Fried Green Tomatoes

Tomatoes were once thought to be poisonous. Over time, people realized that this juicy fruit was safe to eat raw as well as cooked. In this popular African American recipe, **unripe**, or green, tomatoes are fried to make a delicious treat.

 Preparation time: 10 minutes   Servings: 6
Cooking time: 20 minutes

¾ cup (200 ml) cornmeal	pinch of black pepper
⅓ cup (85 ml) flour	4 green tomatoes, sliced
½ teaspoon (3 ml) sugar	3 tablespoons (45 ml)
½ teaspoon (3 ml) salt	cooking oil

1. Combine cornmeal, flour, sugar, salt, and pepper in a bowl. Dip the tomato slices in mixture to coat.
2. Heat oil in a large frying pan. In batches, fry the tomato slices and lightly brown each side.

Rainbow Coleslaw

Most settlers grew cabbage. German settlers shredded and pickled it to make **sauerkraut**. Ukrainian and Polish settlers stuffed the leaves with a rice or meat filling. The Irish added cabbage to a mashed potato dish called colcannon, and all settlers used cabbage to make soup. "Coleslaw" comes from the German word for cabbage. It is a cabbage salad.

 Preparation time: 20 minutes   Servings: 6
Cooking time: none

1 cup (250 ml) shredded green cabbage	1 red onion, sliced
1 cup (250 ml) shredded red cabbage	1 yellow pepper, sliced into thin strips
1 cup (250 ml) grated carrot	handful of chopped parsley
1 stalk celery, chopped into thin slices	¼ cup (60 ml) mayonnaise few drops of lemon juice

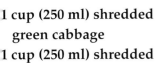

1. With the assistance of an adult, use a food processor to shred and chop the vegetables.
2. Put all the vegetables into a bowl. Toss with the mayonnaise and lemon juice until the coleslaw is well coated with the dressing.

Scotch Broth
"Take half teacup barley; four quarts cold water; bring to the boil and skim; put in now a neck of mutton and boil again for half an hour; skim well the sides, also the pot; have ready two carrots, one large onion, one small head cabbage, one bunch parsley, one sprig celery tops; chop all these fine; add your chopped vegetables, pepper and salt to taste; take two hours to cook."
THE COMPLETE HOME

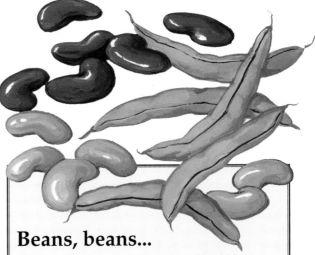

Beans, beans...

Native Americans have been growing beans for thousands of years. Each cultural group that came to North America also used some type of bean for cooking. Beans were filling and nutritious as well as plentiful and inexpensive. When served with rice, they were a good replacement for meat when it was not available. In summer, the pioneers picked beans and cooked them fresh. Extra beans were preserved by pickling or drying. The settlers added dry beans to soups and stews. Sometimes they cooked and flavored beans with bear fat and maple syrup. Some people ground their beans into a paste, which was used to spread on bread. Cowboys enjoyed baked beans for dinner while camping out.

Tremendous tubers

Tubers are root vegetables—they grow in soil. Pioneers planted carrots, beets, potatoes, sweet potatoes, turnips, and parsnips because these tubers were easy to grow. They stored them underground in cellars, where it was cool enough to preserve the tubers but not cold enough to freeze them. Tubers need to be stored out of the sunlight so they will not ripen quickly. Tubers were used in many pioneer recipes because they are hardy, versatile, and delicious! Find all the recipes in this book that contain tubers.

The pioneers cleaned their vegetables thoroughly. They boiled them to remove any dirt or animal droppings as well as insects or other pests.

carrot

Most tubers need to be peeled before they are cooked.

beet

parsnip

sweet potato

Parsnip Soup

This recipe was enjoyed by the French settlers. It is also delicious when made with carrots, turnips, or sweet potatoes. Try making it with your favorite tuber.

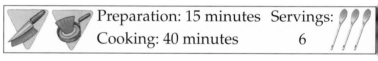

Preparation: 15 minutes   Servings:
Cooking: 40 minutes   6

3 strips bacon	3 cups (750 ml) milk
2 onions, diced	3 tablespoons (45 ml) butter
2 cups (500 ml) parsnips, peeled and diced	1 teaspoon (5 ml) salt
2 cups (500 ml) potatoes, peeled and diced	$1/4$ cup (60 ml) cream
1 cup (250 ml) water	pinch of pepper
	chopped parsley or green onions

1. Cut the bacon into pieces and fry in a pan. Set aside the bacon and leave bacon grease in pan.
2. Fry onions in bacon grease on medium heat for 3 minutes, stirring often.
3. Place parsnips or other tubers and potatoes in a soup pot with the water. Bring to a boil over medium-high heat and cook for about 15 minutes.
4. Test the tubers with a fork. When cooked, turn down the heat and add milk, butter, salt, cream, and cooked onions. Cook 10 minutes on low heat.
5. Serve soup in a bowl and add the pepper. Top with parsley, green onions, and crumbled bacon.

weet-Potato Pie

weet potatoes were not only used in main course
lishes but also in dessert recipes because of their
weet flavor. Sweet-Potato Pie was a popular dessert
nade by the African American settlers.

Preparation time: 20 minutes   Servings: 6
Cooking time: 55 minutes

ne 9 inch (23 cm) pie shell
 cup (250 ml) sweet
  potatoes, peeled, cut into
  chunks, and boiled
 cup (125 ml) brown
  sugar
 cups (180 ml) milk

1 egg, beaten
1 tablespoon (15 ml)
  vegetable oil
¹/₂ teaspoon (3 ml) nutmeg
¹/₂ teaspoon (3 ml) cinnamon
¹/₄ teaspoon (1 ml) each
  baking powder and salt

Preheat oven to 350°F (175°C).

. Beat together the sweet potatoes, brown sugar,
  milk, egg, and oil in a mixing bowl. Add nutmeg,
  cinnamon, baking powder, and salt. Mix well.

. Pour mixture into pie shell. Bake for 55 minutes or
  until a knife inserted in the center comes out clean.

Potato Skins

Potatoes are eaten around the world. The settlers
brought potato recipes from their home countries.

Preparation time: 20 minutes   Servings: 4
Cooking time: 20 minutes

 potatoes, baked, cooled, and sliced in half lengthwise
 tablespoons (30 ml) butter, melted
 strips bacon, cooked and crumbled
 green onion, trimmed and diced
¹/₂ cup (125 ml) grated cheddar cheese

Preheat oven to 400°F (200°C)

1. Scoop much of the potato pulp from each half.
   Leave about half an inch of pulp around the sides.
   Save the scooped potato to make mashed potatoes.

2. Brush the inside of each potato half with butter.
   Sprinkle with bacon, onion, and cheese.

3. Bake in oven for 20 minutes or until cheese
   is melted and bubbling.

To prevent them from rotting, potatoes were dug up as soon as they stopped growing.

You can buy ready-made pie shells at your grocery store.

potato skins

For Mexican-style potato skins, replace the bacon and onion with salsa. Add slices of hot peppers, such as jalapeños.

Discovering corn and wild rice

This young settler is pulling back the husk of a cob of corn to see if it is ready to be harvested.

Native Americans showed the settlers how to grow and cook corn. Corn could be grown on a small area of land. Vegetables such as squash were planted between the rows of corn to save garden space. The large leaves of the low plants shaded the soil from the sun, helping keep the roots moist. Beans were planted beside the corn to use the tall corn stalks for support.

Settlers added corn to soups and stews. They dried and ground it to make cornmeal, which was used to make bread and porridge. Warm kernels of corn covered with milk made a tasty breakfast food. Dried kernels were heated over a fire until they popped open to make popcorn.

Johnny Cake

Some people believe that the name "johnny cake" comes from a Native American name. Others say its name stems from "journey cake." This cake traveled well and lasted for long periods of time because it did not contain butter, milk, or eggs. The batter can be fried in a pan over a fire, but this recipe is baked in the oven.

Preparation time: 15 minutes	Servings: 6
Cooking time: 30 minutes	

1¼ cups (300 ml) flour
¾ cup (180 ml) cornmeal
½ teaspoon (3 ml) salt
2 teaspoon (10 ml) baking powder

1 egg, beaten
1 cup (250 ml) milk
¼ cup (60 ml) melted butter

Preheat oven to 350°F (175°C).
1. Combine flour, cornmeal, salt, and baking powder.
2. Beat together egg, milk, and butter. Stir liquid into dry ingredients.
3. Pour batter into a greased 9x13x2 inch (23x33x5 cm) pan and bake in oven for 30 minutes. Serve warm.

Pioneers fed corn cobs to their pigs. They stuffed husks into mattresses, wove them into rugs, or used them to make toys such as dolls.

Popping Trail Mix

Native Americans introduced popcorn to the settlers. Today popcorn is usually popped in a microwave, but there was a time when all popping was done over a fire on hot coals. Try this recipe and take some with you on walks, car trips, or to school for a snack.

Preparation time: 5 minutes   Servings: 8
Cooking time: none

cup (250 ml) mixed nuts
cup (250 ml) chopped dried fruits
(cherries, raisins, dates, apples)
1/2 cups (375 ml) popped corn

Mix all ingredients together and store in an airtight container or resealable bag to keep fresh.

Wild Rice with Cranberries

The Native Americans who lived in the Great Lakes region of Canada and the United States harvested **wild rice**. It is the grain of a type of grass that grows only in very wet areas. This rice is dark brown in color and, when cooked, it splits and curls and has a nutty flavor.

Preparation time: 10 minutes Servings: 6
Cooking time: 1 hour

cups (1 l) water
cup (250 ml) wild rice
tablespoons (30 ml) olive oil
0 mushrooms, thinly sliced
green onions, diced

1 teaspoon (5 ml) each,
   dried sage and thyme
1/2 cup (125 ml) dried
   cranberries
salt and pepper to taste

. In a large saucepan over high heat, bring water and rice to a boil. Reduce heat to medium and cover pot loosely. Cook until water is absorbed and rice is tender (about 45 to 60 minutes).

2. While rice is cooking, heat oil over medium heat and **sauté** mushrooms until soft. Add onions, sage, thyme, and cranberries. Add a little more oil, if needed, and cook for 3 minutes. Remove from heat.

3. Remove rice from heat and let sit for 5 minutes.

4. Fluff rice with a fork and stir in the mushroom mixture. Serve hot.

The corn that most pioneers ate was yellow, but corn comes in many colors— white, red, and blue!

*A **corn popper** was invented to pop corn kernels over a fire. The long handle allowed its user to stand back from the flames.*

Native American women often harvested the wild rice. They used canoes to reach the plants. Holding onto a bunch of the long grasses, they struck the heads with a small paddle that had sharp edges. The grains of wild rice fell into the canoe. When they finished harvesting the rice, the women dried it on mats that hung over a fire.

Eggs and dairy

*Hens did not lay eggs during the winter, so settlers pickled some eggs to preserve them. Others were dipped in grease and packed in straw for safekeeping. Eggs were also used for **barter**, or trade, at the general store.*

When the pioneers moved to a new area, they brought a few animals with them. Many of the animals provided settlers with a steady supply of food. Pork, bacon, ham, and sausages came from pigs. Cows and goats provided milk, and chickens laid eggs.

Cheese making

To make cheese, the cook heated milk and stirred in **rennet**, which was made from the lining of a calf's stomach. Rennet caused the milk to **curdle**, or thicken. These curds were separated from the watery **whey** and then pressed into a mold to form cheese. The cheese was stored in a cool, dry place for a few months to improve its flavor.

Spanish Omelet

This recipe was a favorite with Mexican cowboys. It can be served mild or spicy, with toast or corn chips.

 Preparation time: 10 minutes   Servings: 2
Cooking time: 10 minutes

The pioneers usually did not drink milk. They used it mainly for making butter and cheese.

3 eggs, lightly beaten	1 tomato, cored and diced
2 tablespoons (30 ml) milk	¼ cup (60 ml) grated
oil for frying	cheddar cheese
¼ cup (60 ml) chopped onion	a few slices of jalapeño
½ green pepper, chopped	(if you dare!)

1. Combine eggs and milk in a bowl and beat lightly.
2. Heat a little oil in a non-stick frying pan. Fry onions and green pepper until they are soft. Stir in tomato and cook for one minute.
3. Pour egg mixture on top of vegetables and let it cook until the bottom starts to form a solid shell.
4. Spread cheese over the omelet and fold in half.
5. Let it cook until the cheese has melted. Put on a plate and garnish with jalapeño pepper slices, corn chips, and salsa.

Other omelet fillings

Immigrants from different countries have their own ways of making omelets. Here are some for you to try:

French: ham and different cheeses
Greek: feta cheese, olives, red onion
         (layer on top of egg mixture)
Chinese: green onions, water chestnuts,
         bean sprouts, mushrooms,
         and shredded pork or chicken

Fabulous fish

Fish provided an abundant food source. The pioneers fished in rivers and streams for trout and salmon and caught bass in lakes. The ocean provided shellfish such as lobster and crab. Most fish could be cooked fresh in a frying pan or as part of a soup. The settlers preserved their fish by salting or smoking it so it could be eaten at a later time. In the late 1800s, foods were preserved in cans. Oysters from the east coast were canned and shipped to the pioneers living inland. They were a popular delicacy saved for special occasions.

Fishing was a popular pastime for both girls and boys. Children often made their own fishing poles.

Fish Cakes

Leftover fish could be used to make fish sticks or fish cakes. They were a favorite treat with pioneer children, just as they are with children today. The fish cakes of the pioneers included leftover fish and mashed potatoes. This recipe uses canned salmon, mayonnaise, and soda crackers. Enjoy your fish cakes with a dandelion salad or rainbow coleslaw.

  Preparation time: 10 minutes   Servings: 2
Cooking time: 10 minutes

one 7¹/₂ ounce (220 ml) can salmon, drained	12 soda crackers
2 tablespoons (30 ml) mayonnaise	1 teaspoon (5 ml) lemon juice
	oil or butter for frying

1. In a bowl, break salmon into pieces with a fork. Add mayonnaise and stir until salmon is coated.
2. Place soda crackers between two pieces of waxed paper and crush with a rolling pin.
3. Add crushed crackers and lemon juice to salmon mixture and stir until well blended.
4. With clean hands, form four flat, round patties.
5. Heat the oil and fry the patties on low heat until they are brown. Flip them over. When the second side is brown, the fish cakes are ready to eat.

Fish Soup

This Asian-style fish soup can be a broth for other soups or served with rice or noodles. Ask an adult for help with chopping and using the stove.

1 pound (450 grams) fish such as bass, trout, salmon, or swordfish, washed
¹/₂ cup (125 ml) fresh cilantro, chopped
1 large onion, diced
4 carrots, diced
2 celery stalks, diced
1 tablespoon (15 ml) soy sauce
¹/₂ teaspoon (3 ml) chili sauce (optional)

1. Put fish into pot with cilantro, carrots, and half the onion. Cover with cold water and simmer ¹/₂ hour.
2. Strain fish and vegetables from the liquid and bring liquid to a boil. Add remaining ingredients.
3. Reduce heat and simmer until celery is cooked. For a heartier soup, add cooked rice or Chinese noodles.

When unexpected guests showed up for dinner, they were often served a **potluck** meal. As guests arrived, the host would add the various foods they brought to the pot hanging over the fire. Often, the meal was a surprise by the time it was cooked.

Pioneers also preserved meat by smoking it. The meat was hung for days over a fire in a small building or hollowed tree trunk.

Meat dishes

Meat was an important part of a settler's diet. A large animal such as a deer provided meat for months. The pioneers also raised animals such as pigs for their meat and fat. To preserve meat or fish, settlers salted it by layering it with salt in a barrel. Stews, soups, and casseroles used only small pieces of meat, allowing the settlers to make their meat supply last.

English Beef Stew

Cooking a stew slowly over the fire all day allowed preserved meat to become tender and easier to chew. This recipe can be changed slightly to make two other kinds of stews—Irish Stew and Hungarian Goulash.

Preparation: 20 minutes
Cooking: 2.5 hours   Servings: 6

3 tablespoon (45 ml) oil	2 cups (500 ml) beef stock
2 large onions, diced	2 cups (500 ml) water
4 garlic cloves, minced	one 16-ounce (475 ml) can
3 stalks celery, sliced	stewed tomatoes
3 carrots, sliced	salt and pepper to taste
1/2 pound (225 grams) stewing beef, cubed	1 tablespoon (15 ml) dried thyme
1/2 cup (125 ml) flour	3 potatoes, peeled and diced

1. In a large stockpot, heat oil over medium heat. Add onions, garlic, celery, and carrots and cook until lightly browned. Stir to prevent burning.
2. Dust meat cubes with flour and add to stockpot. Stir until the meat starts to brown.
3. Add beef stock, water, tomatoes, salt, pepper, and thyme. Cook stew for about 2 hours on low heat.
4. Add potatoes and cook another 20 minutes.

Note: To make Irish Stew, use stewing lamb instead of beef. Flavor with a teaspoon (5 ml) of marjoram. For Hungarian Goulash, use beef or lamb and flavor with paprika and parsley instead of thyme.

Shepherd's Pie

This British dish was often made with leftover potatoes. Greek immigrants made a dish very similar called *moussaka*. In addition to the ingredients below, *moussaka* also contains eggplant and tomato paste.

Preparation time: 15 minutes
Cooking time: 1 hour   Servings: 6

oil for frying
1 medium onion, chopped
1 pound (450 g) ground beef
1½ cup (375 ml) mixed frozen vegetables

2 cups (500 ml) mashed potatoes
½ cup (125 ml) grated cheddar cheese (optional)

Preheat oven to 350°F (175°C).

1. Heat oil in a frying pan over medium heat. Sauté onion until soft. Add beef and cook until brown.
2. Transfer cooked beef and onion to a greased 8-inch (20 cm) square casserole dish. Layer the mixed vegetables over the beef and top with the mashed potatoes. Sprinkle with cheese, if desired.
3. Bake 40 minutes or until top is a golden color.

Oven Fried Chicken

For a full meal, serve this recipe with the Wild Rice with Cranberries (see page 19). After handling raw chicken, wash your hands and all surfaces well.

Preparation time: 10 minutes   Servings: 4
Cooking time: 20 minutes

4 skinless, boneless chicken breasts
1 egg
2 tablespoons (30 ml) water

½ cup (125 ml) finely crushed cornflakes
salt and pepper to taste

Preheat oven to 450°F (225°C).

1. Wash chicken well and pat dry.
2. Whisk egg and water in a flat-bottomed bowl.
3. Combine cornflakes and seasonings in a plastic bag.
4. Dip the chicken in egg mixture. Place in bag with cornflake mixture and shake until coated.
5. Put chicken on a greased baking sheet and bake for 20 minutes or until chicken is cooked through.

Shepherds tended sheep in the fields. Originally, the meat from these animals was used in Shepherd's Pie.

A roasting kitchen was placed inside the fireplace. One side of the metal box was open and faced the flames. The cook could check the meat and baste it using a door on the other side.

27

Tempting treats

Early settlers had only an open fire and a few pots with which to cook. They often made puddings for dessert by simply boiling the ingredients in a pot over the fire. In later years, bread ovens were used to bake pies. Fruits in season such as apples and berries made tasty pie fillings and toppings for other desserts. Cakes were baked only for special occasions because they required expensive ingredients.

Native Pudding

Pioneers and Native Americans introduced each other to various new foods. The settlers brought foods from Europe such as apples, dairy products, and wheat flour. Native Americans introduced the pioneers to the foods that existed only in North America, including corn, pumpkins, and maple syrup. Over time, these foods were used in meals made by both Native Americans and the settlers.

Preparation time: 10 minutes	Servings: 8
Cooking time: 1.5 hours	

2 cups (500 ml) milk
1/2 cup (125 ml) cornmeal
2 cups (500 ml) apple cider
2 tablespoons (30 ml) butter, melted
1/2 cup (125 ml) molasses
1 teaspoon (5 ml) salt
1 teaspoon (5 ml) cinnamon
2 eggs, beaten
1/2 cup (125 ml) raisins

Preheat oven to 325°F (175°C)
1. Heat milk in a saucepan over low heat. Do not boil.
2. In a bowl, stir the cornmeal into the cider and slowly stir into the milk.
3. Cook mixture over medium-low heat, stirring continuously until thickened (about 20 minutes). Remove from heat.
4. Combine remaining ingredients in a bowl. Whisk in milk mixture. Pour batter into a greased 9x13x2 inch (23x33x5 cm) pan and bake in oven for one hour.

Some settlers grew fruit trees such as cherry, apple, and pear. The trees were planted soon after the land was cleared. It often took years for the trees to bear plenty of fruit.

In addition to eating fresh apples, pioneers used them to make apple cider and a sweetener called fructose.

German Baked Apples

Apples were a favorite fruit of the pioneers. They could be stored for long periods of time. The pioneers used them in main dishes, desserts, snacks, beverages, and spreads. Apples were not only tasty but also nutritious!

 Preparation time: 15 minutes   Servings: 4
Cooking time: 20 minutes

large apples
teaspoons (20 ml) brown sugar or maple syrup
raisins, cinnamon, chopped nuts or dried fruit (optional)
cup (125 ml) water

Preheat oven to 350°F (175°C).

. Wash apples. Have an adult core the apples, leaving ½ inch (1 cm) remaining at bottom. Score the skin all around, 1 inch (2 cm) from top.

.. Mix brown sugar with raisins or other optional ingredients. Using a spoon, fill the center of each apple. Place the apples in an oven-proof dish and pour water into the dish.

. Bake in oven for 20 minutes or until the top of each apple rises.

Spoon the sugar, nut, and fruit mixture into the apple a little at a time.

The baked apple tastes just like pudding when it is done. For dessert, top with ice cream or whipped cream. For breakfast, eat plain or with yogurt.

Strawberry Shortcakes

This traditional summertime treat can now be enjoyed at any time of the year. Today's store-bought shortcakes and fruit make this recipe quick and easy to make. Try topping the shortcake with other fruits such as raspberries or blueberries or even a combination of kiwis and bananas!

Preparation time: 10 minutes   Servings: 6
Cooking time: none

shortcake cups or scones
cups (500 ml) strawberries, washed, cored, and sliced
cups (750 ml) whipped cream

Fill each cup with strawberries, or slice the scones in half and place strawberries inside. Top with a big spoonful of whipped cream. Enjoy!

Using scones, this tasty treat also makes a nourishing breakfast.

Most settlers did not have running water in their home. They carried heavy buckets of water long distances from a spring or creek. Eventually, a well was dug, and the settlers could fetch water just outside their door.

To collect the sap from a maple tree, settlers drilled a hole into the trunk and inserted a spout from which the sap would drip.

Beverages

The settlers made most of their beverages with ingredients already available to them. The leaves, roots, and flowers of many herbs and other plants were used to make tea. Fruits were crushed and used to make hot and cold drinks. Some pioneers roasted roots or beans to brew beverages. Coffee and cocoa could be purchased at the general store, but they were costly and used only on special occasions.

Hot Apple Cider Punch

Apple cider was made in the autumn, after apples were harvested. The cider kept well in a cool place for much of the winter.

Preparation time: 5 minutes	Servings: 6
Cooking time: 30 minutes	

2 quarts (2 l) apple cider
½ cup (125 ml) sugar
3 cinnamon sticks

2 teaspoons (10 ml) whole cloves

1. In a pot, heat cider, sugar, cinnamon, and cloves until the mixture is boiling.
2. Cover and simmer for a half hour.
3. Strain and pour into a punch bowl.

Maple Lemonade

Native Americans have a long tradition of collecting the sap from maple trees and boiling it down to make syrup and sugar. When the settlers arrived, maple syrup and sugar were traded for other goods.

Maple Lemonade is a simple but refreshing drink to make. Add 2 tablespoons (30 ml) of maple syrup to 1 cup (250 ml) of cold water. Add ice cubes and squeeze the juice of a wedge of lemon into a glass. For a warming winter treat, add the maple syrup to hot water. You can serve this drink with a stick of cinnamon and a slice of lemon.

Cooking terms

baste To moisten meat while cooking with a liquid such as drippings or melted butter

batter A thick liquid mixture consisting of ingredients such as eggs, milk, and flour

beat To mix a liquid or soft paste rapidly

blend To mix several ingredients together

chop To cut into tiny, fine pieces using a knife or food processor

core To remove the seeds and woody stem from fruit such as apples or pears

cornstarch A soft powder made from corn grains

crane A swinging iron bar inside a fireplace from which pots were hung over the fire

dice To cut food into tiny cubes using a knife

drippings Juices and fat that are secreted by meat or poultry as it roasts

Dutch oven A large covered pot used for baking breads, rolls, biscuits, and stews

fructose A type of sugar found naturally in fruit such as apples

fry To cook food over high heat with oil or butter

grate To cut foods into small, thin pieces by rubbing them against a grater

grease To coat a pan with oil or melted butter

knead The act of mixing and smoothing out dough before it is baked

mince To chop very finely using a food processor

mix To combine ingredients in a bowl or pot

open-faced Describing a sandwich with one slice of bread upon which toppings are placed

peel The act of removing the skin of a fruit or vegetable, using a knife or peeler

pinch A measurement of an ingredient based on the amount held between the tips of two fingers

preserves Fruit that has been cooked with sugar and stored in a jar to prevent it from spoiling

purée To chop a solid food in a food processor until it has become smooth

rise To swell before cooking, as in dough

rub in To mix ingredients together using fingers

sauté To fry food lightly over medium heat with oil

score To make shallow cuts on the surface of food

shred To cut food into small, fine slices using a knife or food processor

sieve A mesh bowl used to separate solids from liquid or to sift powders such as flour

skim To remove floating solids or fat from the top of a liquid

slice To cut food into pieces of even size

strain The act of separating solids from liquids

whip The act of beating food, usually eggs or cream, into a light foam

whisk (n) A utensil used to whip food; (v) The act of whipping food

Index

5 6 7 8 9 0   Printed in U.S.A.   9 8 7 6 5